1ONE

CONFRONTING
THE **OBSTACLE**
BETWEEN YOU
AND **CHRIST**

PAUL SCHWANKE

THING

Copyright © 2013 by Striving Together Publications.
All Scripture quotations are taken from
the King James Version.

First published in 2013 by Striving Together Publications, a ministry
of Lancaster Baptist Church, Lancaster, CA 93535. Striving Together
Publications is committed to providing tried, trusted, and proven
resources that will further equip local churches to carry out the
Great Commission. Your comments and suggestions are valued.

All rights reserved. No part of this book may be reproduced, stored
in a retrieval system, or transmitted in any form or by any means—
electronic, mechanical, photocopy, recording, or otherwise—
without written permission of the publisher, except for brief
quotations in printed reviews.

Striving Together Publications
4020 E. Lancaster Blvd.
Lancaster, CA 93535
800.201.7748
www.strivingtogether.com

Cover design by Andrew Hutchens
Layout by Craig Parker
Edited by Sarah Browning
Special thanks to our proofreaders

The author and publication team have put forth every effort to give proper
credit to quotes and thoughts that are not original with the author. It is not
our intent to claim originality with any quote or thought that could not
readily be tied to an original source.

ISBN 978-1-59894-229-3
Printed in the United States of America

Contents

Introduction

Standing before the Lord Jesus Christ was a rich, young ruler. The smooth talking, fame-hungry ministers of our day would have been ecstatic. A handsome, young politician would be the perfect addition to any platform. He certainly could help in building a massive crowd and, of course, he couldn't hurt the love offering.

Not having a moral compass wouldn't be so bad considering the perks. Think of the invitations for golf—private meetings with politicians and, if played well, maybe even opening in prayer for the Inauguration.

But Jesus didn't see this rich ruler as most would. He saw the man differently. Mark 10:21 shares, "Then Jesus beholding him loved him." Jesus did not love his wallet. He did not love his personality. He did not love his position. Jesus did not love what He could get from the man or even what the man could do for Him. Jesus loved *him*.

There was a lot to admire about this young politician. He came "running" to Jesus; he "kneeled to him," and showed the greatest of respect by calling him "Good Master" (Mark 10:17). In our present day, the sad truth is that many only know the name of Jesus as a name to be profaned, ridiculed, or denied. It would be difficult to find someone actually running to Jesus and kneeling in His presence in our day. This young politician had an apparent respect for Jesus. So far, so good.

Next came a question that sincere, religious people have perpetually raised from the beginning of time, *"What shall I do that I may inherit eternal life?"*

In other words, "I want to go to Heaven. There must be *something* I can do to get there. Just name it."

Religious people have been trying to impress God for centuries. The Buddhist lights his candles and burns his incense. The Muslim prays to Mecca. The Catholic confesses his sins to the priest. The Hindu makes a pilgrimage to the Ganges River. The Lutheran is confirmed. And the Baptist says a prayer.

"There must be something I can do to impress God. There must be some way I can make myself good enough for Heaven. There must be something I can give, something I can pray, somewhere I can go, but I need to know what it is. *What shall I do that I may inherit eternal life?*"

The answer from Jesus is unexpected. One might expect a grand religious discourse with flowery language and astute philosophy, but that was not His way. There is a reason the "common people heard him gladly" (Mark 12:37).

Jesus spoke simply, "Thou knowest the commandments" (Mark 10:19). He informed the rich, young ruler that if he indeed wanted to *do* something to inherit eternal life, then he'd better be certain to keep the holy commands of God. Jesus even helped him by listing seven of them. "…Thou shalt do no murder, Thou shalt not commit adultery, Thou shalt not steal, Thou shalt not bear false witness, Honour thy father and thy mother: and, Thou shalt love thy neighbour as thyself" (Matthew 19:18–19).

The ball was in the court of our young friend. He was face to face with the demands of God's law which required perfection. And truthfully, no honest person could ever read that holy law and claim to be spotless. God's simple declaration is that "all have sinned" (Romans 3:23). Yet, incredibly, the ruler tells Jesus, "All these have I observed from my youth" (Mark 10:20).

Clearly, he was not able to deceive the Son of God, for Jesus "knew what was in [him]" (John 2:25). But instead of instigating a debate or an argument, Jesus simply went to the heart of the matter. He broke through the smokescreen of religious argument, He saw through the facade of sacred self-righteousness, and He extinguished the raging fire of human pride with four simple words.

"One thing thou lackest."

"One thing!" Not a thousand things, not a hundred things, not even a dozen things, but rather, *one thing* was keeping this man out of Heaven.

"Sir, you don't need a pilgrimage. You don't need a confession. You don't need a baptistry. You don't need a minister. You don't need a religion. But there is *one thing* that you must deal with."

The young ruler was about to learn that Jesus and religion are incompatible. Religion always produces a tedious list of do's and don'ts, creating a system of complexity. The common man then is convinced that he needs a minister, rabbi, preacher, priest, monk, elder, imam, or TV evangelist before he can even get started.

Jesus wrapped it into a nice four-word package that was simple enough for anyone to understand: *"One thing thou lackest."*

One thing was keeping this man out of Heaven.

Jesus continues, "Go thy way, sell whatsoever thou hast, and give to the poor, and thou shalt have treasure in heaven: and come, take up the cross, and follow me"

(Mark 10:21). In twenty-eight understandable words, Jesus brings the man to a point of decision.

The reaction is noticeable on two fronts. First, our rich, young ruler was "sad" and "grieved." The word *sad* means "to be overcast," a word in the Bible that refers to a gloomy, cloudy day. His response was immediately written across his face. He never spoke with his tongue, but he certainly did with his eyes.

Then, with a heart full of sorrow, he turns and walks away. That would not work for him. Maybe he expected a softened response from Christ, honoring his goodness and stature. Perhaps there was a political favor he could do for the Lord. Conceivably, had Jesus told him to make a contribution to the ministry, he would have quickly reached for his checkbook.

But Jesus did not ask for a *contribution*. He said, *sell it all.*

As quickly as he came, he went away. And the rich, young ruler disappeared from the pages of the Bible— gone for good—all because of *one thing.*

There is another response to observe. As the disciples watched these proceedings, Jesus gave the commentary: "How hardly shall they that have riches enter into the kingdom of God!" (Mark 10:23).

The Bible says the followers of Christ were "astonished." They were *so* astonished that Jesus repeated Himself. "How hard is it for them that trust in riches to enter into the kingdom of God!" He went on to tell them it was "easier for a camel to go through the eye of a needle, than for a rich man to enter into the kingdom of God" (Mark 10:24–25).

This time the disciples were "astonished out of measure," a step beyond plain, old, ordinary astonishment. The phrase means they were knocked out of their senses, clubbed by a spiritual two-by-four.

Jesus had been teaching them about salvation. It is by "grace...through faith" (Ephesians 2:8). Forgiveness is for "him that worketh not" (Romans 4:5). To go to Heaven, a sinner must understand that it is "not by works of righteousness" (Titus 3:5).

Yet Jesus seemed to be contradicting the Bible. Is eternal life the "gift of God" (Romans 6:23), or is it for sale? Is salvation for "as many as received him" (John 1:12), or is it for as many as take a vow of poverty? Is salvation for those who "call upon the name of the Lord" (Romans 10:13), or is it for those who empty their bank accounts?

No wonder those disciples were "astonished."

But Jesus went on, "How hard is it for them that trust in riches to enter into the kingdom of God!" For the rich, young ruler, the *one thing* was a choice. "Do I trust in my riches or do I trust in Jesus?" There was no room for both. Before he could ever go to Heaven, he had to decide where his confidence would lie.

One decision. One choice. One roadblock. *One thing.*

Many people miss Heaven because of *one thing.* Regardless of life's issues and complications, they have one thing keeping them from Christ. That one thing certainly varies in every person's life. It might be a sinful pleasure, a misplaced priority, or a dirty habit. It might be another person or an enjoyable hobby. It might be written across the person's life so that everyone can see it, or it may be so well hidden in a man's soul that only God and the individual know it is there. But for so many people, there is one thing that keeps them from trusting Christ fully.

Walk with me through the Bible as we visit three individuals who had one thing that had to be dealt with. Watch the Saviour bring them to a place of decision where they responded to God's wonderful call. Listen to Him tenderly plead in your own heart over the *one thing* that may be keeping you from Christ.

One thing.

Will it be the one thing, or will it be Christ?

Chapter One

NICODEMUS
Enslaved by Religion

The shuffling feet of the honored man broke the silence of the night. He had an appointment to keep with Jesus in hopes that a myriad of his questions might be answered. Little could he imagine how his life was about to change. Doctor Nicodemus, the esteemed "master of Israel," was going to conference with the One who surpassed all religion. Nicodemus knew *about* God, but Jesus *knew* God. Nicodemus knew what was in the books and the scrolls, but Jesus knew "what was in man" (John 2:25). Nicodemus saw the "miracles which he did" (John 2:23), but Jesus saw the real Nicodemus. A conversation between a man who can look on the "outward appearance" and the Lord who "looketh on the heart" (1 Samuel 16:7) could quickly become a one-sided dialogue.

Consider the story of Nicodemus in John 3:

There was a man of the Pharisees, named Nicodemus, a ruler of the Jews: The same came to Jesus by night, and said unto him, Rabbi, we know that thou art a teacher come from God: for no man can do these miracles that thou doest, except God be with him. Jesus answered and said unto him, Verily, verily, I say unto thee, Except a man be born again, he can not see the kingdom of God. Nicodemus saith unto him, How can a man be born when he is old? can he enter the second time into his mother's womb, and be born? Jesus answered, Verily, verily, I say unto thee, Except a man be born of water and of the Spirit, he can not enter into the kingdom of God. That which is born of the flesh is flesh; and that which is born of the Spirit is spirit. Marvel not that I said unto thee, Ye must be born again. The wind bloweth where it listeth, and thou hearest the sound thereof, but canst not tell whence it cometh, and whither it goeth: so is every one that is born of the Spirit. Nicodemus answered and said unto him, How can these things be? Jesus answered and said unto him, Art thou a master of Israel, and knowest not these things? Verily, verily, I say unto thee, We speak that we do know, and testify that we have seen; and ye receive not our witness. If I have told you earthly things, and ye believe not, how shall ye believe, if I tell you of heavenly things? And no man hath ascended up to heaven, but he that came down from heaven, even the Son of man which is in heaven.

And as Moses lifted up the serpent in the wilderness, even so must the Son of man be lifted up: That whosoever believeth in him should not perish, but have eternal life.

For God so loved the world, that he gave his only begotten Son, that whosoever believeth in him should not perish, but have everlasting life. For God sent not his Son into the world to condemn the world; but that the world through him might be saved.

He that believeth on him is not condemned: but he that believeth not is condemned already, because he hath not believed in the name of the only begotten Son of God.And this is the condemnation, that light is come into the world, and men loved darkness rather than light, because their deeds

were evil. For every one that doeth evil hateth
the light, neither cometh to the light, lest his
deeds should be reproved. But he that doeth
truth cometh to the light, that his deeds may be
made manifest, that they are wrought in God.
—JOHN 3:1–21

There are few components of a man's life that are
as blinding as religion. When religious antagonists
sneered at Jesus asking, "Are we blind also?" the
Saviour responded, "If ye were blind, ye should have
no sin: but now ye say, We see; therefore your sin
remaineth" (John 9:40–41). There is a difference
between a blind man who knows he cannot see and
a blind person who thinks he can. Multitudes of
people in spiritual darkness doubtlessly approached
Nicodemus over the years for his insights, yet
Nicodemus was as blind as they were. Before he could
see and be saved, Jesus had to confront the great
obstacle in the life of Nicodemus—he was blinded
by religion.

He had to deal with his *one thing*. He had to decide, "Do I want my religion or do I want the Saviour?"

A man who only sees the inside of a church at weddings and funerals has no comprehension of Nicodemus' struggle. He cannot understand the hold that religion has over individuals, the guilt of failing to meet religious standards, and the terror of excommunication.

But a person entrenched in religion has a different view of Nicodemus' story in John 3. Nicodemus may have attended a religious school, had a family heritage intertwined with his church, or had an emotional attachment that reached the depths of his soul. When Nicodemus visited Christ, at stake was his reputation, his income, and his family standing. The man must have been searching.

Yet for all the complexity and confusion that religion brings, Jesus brought it all down to *one thing*. Nicodemus was confronted with a choice—will I trust my religion or will I trust Christ? This would not be a simple decision for Nicodemus, considering what religion had done for him.

Religion made Nicodemus a powerful man.

As a "ruler of the Jews," he was a prominent member of society belonging to an organization called the Sanhedrin. The Sanhedrin was a council consisting of seventy-one men that included priests, elders, and teachers of the law. Its leader was the high priest of Israel himself. Their reach went far beyond religious issues of the day extending to civil, and in some cases, criminal matters. Nicodemus is further described in verse 10 as a "master of Israel," making him a leading teacher in a land full of teachers.

Religion had bestowed its honors and degrees upon the Reverend Doctor Nicodemus. He would be invited to the "uppermost rooms at feasts," be regaled with the "chief seats in the synagogues," and hear the adoring cries of "Rabbi, Rabbi" (Matthew 23:6–7) as he strolled through the market. Life was good in the city of Jerusalem for such a man. He had risen through the ranks, and religion had honored its own. There are very few institutions on earth that can bestow honor and degree like religion can.

But God saw Nicodemus differently than his theologian friends did. God saw him differently than the fawning multitudes did. When God introduces Nicodemus in Scripture, He simply states, "There was a man…." That's it. He was simply a man. The robes did not impress God. The titles did not impress God. The degrees did not impress God. The prayers did not impress God. The sermons did not impress God.

"There was a man." Nicodemus was no different in the eyes of Christ than the "impotent…blind, halt, withered" (John 5:3) people He met. Though the bright lights of religion with its impressive and intimidating culture tend to blind us, Christ was not blinded. Strip away the ornaments of religion, and you will find an ordinary human with very real issues and very real battles. The bedazzled assemblies saw a brilliant orator of majestic esteem, but Jesus saw something else when He looked at Nicodemus.

He was just "a man."

Religion made Nicodemus a fearful man.

The Bible says he "came to Jesus by night." Nicodemus had a reputation to uphold. Everyone expected him to be a man of answers, not questions. In their eyes, Jesus was supposed to seek the approval of the Sanhedrin, but here Nicodemus was seeking Him. With his reputation at stake, Nicodemus could not be too careful, and so he made the journey under the cover of darkness.

Identifying with Christ was a dangerous proposition for a man like Nicodemus. Then (as now) there were numerous "secret disciples" who "believed on him [Jesus]; but because of the Pharisees they did not confess him, lest they should be put out of the synagogue: For they loved the praise of men more than the praise of God" (John 12:42–43). If Nicodemus were somehow seen with Christ, there could be repercussions that might affect his career. It was a far safer proposition to slip out of the city unseen by the probing eyes of the critics, than to risk meeting Christ in daylight.

Religious people must always look over their shoulders. Their reputations depend on the opinions of the hierarchy. They live with a relentless anxiety as to how they are seen by others and how they are meeting the expectations that others have placed upon them. Indeed, the "fear of man bringeth a snare" (Proverbs 29:25).

The book *Fifty Years in the Church of Rome* tells the powerful story of Charles Chiniquy. Ordained as a Catholic priest in 1833, he labored in Quebec before moving to Illinois to work with French speaking Catholics. As a young man, his father had instilled in his heart a reverence and devotion for the Bible, which would eventually become the great contention in his life. Would he follow the Bible or the dictates of the Catholic hierarchy?

Someone may consider that an easy choice, but it was not so easy for an individual whose entire life was consumed by religion. Catholicism was Chiniquy's life, his income, and his security. It was not simply a Sunday morning experience for him. It dominated

him. And he understood the cost of leaving his religion
for Christ:

> I felt that an implacable war was to be declared
> against me, which would end only with my
> life. The Pope, the bishops, and priests, all over
> the world, would denounce and curse me. They
> would attack and destroy my character, my name,
> and my honour, in their press, from their pulpit,
> and in their confessionals, where the man they
> strike can never know whence the blow is coming!
> Almost in despair, I tried to think of someone
> who would come to my help in that formidable
> conflict, but could find none. Every one of the
> millions of Roman Catholics were bound to curse
> me. My best friends, my own people, even my
> own brothers, were bound to look upon me with
> horror as an apostate, a vile outcast![1]

The contention found its way to the courtroom,
where slanderous charges were miraculously overcome
in part by the work of his lawyer, Abraham Lincoln.
The conflicts mounted until the Bishop of Rome
announced that he and his parish members "could
no longer be Roman Catholics, if [they] persisted in

putting the Word of God and the gospel of Christ as the foundation of [their] religion, [their] faith and [their] submission."

His choice became clear:

> I did not hesitate. Nothing could induce me to give up the gospel of Christ; and so I gave up the title and position of priest in the Roman Catholic Church. I would rather suffer a thousand deaths than renounce the gospel of Christ. I am no longer a priest of Rome; but I am more than ever a disciple of Christ, a follower of the gospel.[2]

Through the corridor of time, countless multitudes like Mr. Chiniquy could join Nicodemus with their own stories of the fear and control that religion held over their souls.

Religion made Nicodemus a confused man.

In his encounter with Christ, the first word Nicodemus utters is "Rabbi," a term which indicated that Nicodemus recognized Jesus as an equal. To his colleagues, such an appellation would have been considered magnanimous, because in the religious circles of the Pharisees, being a teacher was considered the ultimate position of respect. The Pharisees' studied opinion of Jesus caused them to marvel, "How knoweth this man letters, having never learned?" (John 7:15). Their constant stream of criticism indicated an intense distaste of everything Jesus stood for, and there was no room in their fraternity for Him. Nicodemus was willing to climb out on a lonely limb and recognize Him as a teacher worthy of respect, yet that designation fell woefully short.

Christ was not his equal. Christ was his Creator.

Nicodemus was willing to go much further than the rest of his cohorts in identifying Christ, but he did not go far enough! Religion never does. It is so concerned with straddling the fence and being politically correct, that it fails to take the right stand.

Rabbi was not the proper word. *Christ* was the proper word.

Nicodemus was wise enough to recognize that "God… [was] with him [Christ]," but he failed to see that the "Word [Jesus] was God" (John 1:1).

Religion confused Nicodemus about the paramount kingdom. The Pharisees joined the citizens of Jerusalem in craving a kingdom free from the persecution and harassment of Rome and its emperors. They were tired of paying taxes and tired of foreign intrusion into their affairs. When Jesus preached of a spiritual kingdom that was "within you" (Luke 17:21), even an astute sage like Nicodemus could only question in amazement, "How can these things be?"

The deeper someone goes into the maze of religion, the more complicated life becomes. Listen to the average liberal minister of our day! The longer he speaks, the more baffled the congregation becomes. By the time he reaches the conclusion of his sermon, he has created more questions than answers. Few remember what he said, and fewer still understood what he said.

Listen to the seminary professor! He pontificates from his lectern such profundities that have no impact upon a life. When the semester is completed, the classroom is full of students with many questions yet no answers.

If you asked, "How can I go to Heaven?" many ministers would offer quotes, commands, sermons, rhetoric, philosophy, psychology, and a lot of high-sounding gibberish, but at the end of the conversation, the unstated answer would simply be, "I don't know how to go to Heaven. No one can know they are going to Heaven."

On the surface, wouldn't it seem that this is the reason we have ministers, churches, religions and the like? There are many services that religious organizations perform to assist society, but isn't the primary purpose of religion to get us ready for the day we die?

How different the theologians are from Christ. When we ask Him how to go to Heaven, He responds with five simple words:

"Ye must be born again."

So much for confusion!

Religion made Nicodemus an arrogant man.

Nicodemus informs the Son of God, "we know that thou art a teacher come from God: for no man can do these miracles that thou doest, except God be with him." He says, it is true because "we know." We are the authority; we determine truth; and we will use our cogitation, our consensus, and our conclusions to determine right. It must be so because we have said it is so.

Jesus had a different view of truth. The first words He said were, "Verily, verily," words that simply meant "truly, truly." To Nicodemus, religious teachings were truth. To Jesus, the Word of God was truth.

The challenge that faced Nicodemus is a challenge for all religious people. A choice must be made concerning authority. What is truth?

Most "Christian" religions will claim that the Bible is a great authority, but when pressed, it is not the greatest authority. The Bible is important but so are the words of Joseph Smith. The Bible is revered until it contradicts the Watchtower. The Bible is a book of great truth, but when the Pope speaks *ex cathedra* ("from the throne"), those words are supreme.

Many others believe the Bible is an authority, implying that there are other authorities, but the Bible will be the final, supreme referee in matters. Religion has creeds, decrees, and confessions, but the Bible supersedes them.

Another view, held by Baptists, claims the Bible is not just *an* authority—it is the *only* authority. We do not go to the Bible to settle the arguments; we go to the Bible before the argument begins. It is not the Bible plus the creed, nor the Bible plus the pronouncement, nor the Bible plus the dogmas; it is the Bible and only the Bible.

> ...*thy word is truth.*—JOHN 17:17

> *The words of the LORD are pure words: As silver tried in a furnace of earth, purified seven times. Thou shalt keep them, O LORD, Thou shalt preserve them from this generation for ever.*—PSALM 12:6–7

> *The law of the LORD is perfect, converting the soul: The testimony of the LORD is sure, making wise the*

simple. The statutes of the LORD are right, rejoicing the heart: The commandment of the LORD is pure, enlightening the eyes. The fear of the LORD is clean, enduring for ever: The judgments of the LORD are true and righteous altogether.—PSALM 19:7–9

Thy righteousness is an everlasting righteousness, And thy law is the truth.—PSALM 119:142

Thou art near, O LORD; And all thy commandments are truth.—PSALM 119:151

Thy word is true from the beginning: And every one of thy righteous judgments endureth for ever.—PSALM 119:160

But I will shew thee that which is noted in the scripture of truth: and there is none that holdeth with me in these things, but Michael your prince.—DANIEL 10:21

In whom ye also trusted, after that ye heard the word of truth, the gospel of your salvation: in whom also after that ye believed, ye were sealed with that holy Spirit of promise,—EPHESIANS 1:13

Study to shew thyself approved unto God, a workman that needeth not to be ashamed, rightly dividing the word of truth.—2 TIMOTHY 2:15

Certainly, religion had done a lot for Nicodemus, but it had not done enough. His meeting with Christ would change that. Like an expert surgeon, the Saviour used the scalpel of the Word of God to lay bare the heart and soul of Mr. Religion.

Jesus exposed Nicodemus' faulty reasoning.

Nicodemus, consumed by human thinking, said "no man can do these miracles that thou doest, except God be with him." To him, Jesus must have had a presence with God because of the miracles He was performing. In other words, "God must be with You because I see what You do."

How dangerous the path Nicodemus was walking! Through the centuries people have been convinced that religious charlatans must be right with God because of the miracles they perform. Oral Roberts, Kenneth Copeland, Benny Hinn, Peter Popoff, and their ilk fill stadiums with gullible people who let their emotions be their guide. They think they are witnessing diseases departing from bodies, bad habits magically disappearing, and other maladies being corrected.

But God's truth says, "Beloved, believe not every spirit, but try the spirits whether they are of God: because many false prophets are gone out into the world" (1 John 4:1). "But there were false prophets also among the people, even as there shall be false teachers among you, who privily shall bring in damnable heresies, even denying the Lord that bought them, and bring upon themselves swift destruction" (2 Peter 2:1). "Beware of false prophets, which come to you in sheep's clothing, but inwardly they are ravening wolves" (Matthew 7:15).

Religion looks on the outward appearance, and as long as the outward seems right, religion concludes that all must be right.

Jesus was concerned about a different, deeper type of vision. He told Nicodemus in John 3:3, "Verily, verily, I say unto thee, Except a man be born again, he cannot see the kingdom of God." The word *see* is not

referring to our physical field of vision, but rather our
spiritual vision. It means to perceive and realize and
know. When we are trying to grasp a concept, we will
often use the phrase, "Now, I see." This is the intent of
verse 3.

Religion sits at the superficial end of the spectrum.
Because experience is the ultimate authority, the
mantra becomes, "I see; therefore I believe." But our
experiences can easily be manipulated. Unscrupulous
ministers will say and do anything, and our own
hearts are "deceitful above all things, and desperately
wicked" (Jeremiah 17:9). We cannot know or trust our
own hearts, let alone the heart of a distant minister.

Instead of "I see; therefore I believe," we must
claim, "The Bible says; therefore I believe." Until a
man is born into God's family, he will be blinded and
confused by myriad religious teachings that abound.
A man outside of God's family sees with his eyes and
builds his belief system. A man born into God's family
sees with a spiritual set of eyes through the spectrum
of God's Word. The difference is immense.

Nicodemus needed a new set of eyes!

Jesus exposed Nicodemus' family problem.

Nicodemus was in a quandary that religion could not fix. The problem was not his religious associations, his place of worship, his denomination, nor the school he attended. The problem was not the government, the emperor in Rome, the political situation, nor the fiscal climate. The problem was not his wife, his children, his neighbor, nor the family dog.

Nicodemus was in the wrong family. And until he became a part of the right family, he could not go to Heaven.

Jesus told him, "Ye must be born again." How difficult it must have been for Nicodemus to accept the fact that he belonged to his "father the devil" (John 8:44). From a young age, his life had been dominated by his religion. He had attended the schools, followed the rules, and submitted to religion's authority. If anyone was good enough to go to Heaven, Nicodemus must have thought it was he.

His religious training had become his worst enemy. It kept him from seeing himself as God saw him. Religion cons a man into looking on the outward appearance, convincing him that the robes of external righteousness, which look so good in the mirror of conventional thinking, must be as impressive to God as they are to humans. But God calls those righteous acts "filthy rags" (Isaiah 64:6). The plaudits, the praises, the prestige bestowed in the name of devotion simply prevent a man from seeing himself as God sees him.

> *He that committeth sin is of the devil; for the devil sinneth from the beginning. For this purpose the Son of God was manifested, that he might destroy the works of the devil. Whosoever is born of God doth not commit sin; for his seed remaineth in him: and he cannot sin, because he is born of God. In this the children of God are manifest, and the children of the devil: whosoever doeth not righteousness is not of God, neither he that loveth not his brother.*
> —1 John 3:8–10

Nicodemus might as well compare himself with drunks in the alley, the harlot on the street, the publican in the tax office, and see himself in a good light. Religion is fond of making such comparisons, yet the Bible strictly warns, "For we dare not make ourselves of the number, or compare ourselves with some that commend themselves: but they measuring themselves by themselves, and comparing themselves among themselves, are not wise" (2 Corinthians 10:12).

Nicodemus' problem was not a complex one. There was no reason to be shocked or angered. Jesus told him, "marvel not," because his problem was basic. He was a member of the wrong family, and until he experienced a change of family, Nicodemus could never enter into the kingdom of God. To be a part of God's spiritual family, the kingdom of the saved, he had to be born again.

"Ye must be born again." So simple, yet so complex.

Like so many, Nicodemus was looking for something other than the path of faith, and so Jesus took him to the blowing wind. We have never seen the wind, yet we can see the consequences of the wind. We can see the swaying trees, the rippling flag, the passing clouds, and we know the wind is blowing. We can see the havoc of the tornado and the hurricane, and recognize its power.

Similarly, a person born of the Spirit of God requires faith. There are no human words to explain it, and there is no basis for the feeble, fleshly, human mind to grasp it. For Nicodemus, this must have been an incredibly high mountain to traverse, yet Christ was explaining without apology that "without faith it is impossible to please him" (Hebrews 11:6).

Christ had brought Nicodemus to a critical point of decision. It was time to deal with his *one thing*. It was Christ versus his religion. The compassionate, merciful Son of God had in His tender yet unswayable manner, brought Nicodemus to a place where he must "choose...this day" (Joshua 24:15) where he would place his trust.

I have seen multitudes of people during revival meetings stand as Nicodemus did. The Saviour, the Spirit of God, and the Word of God have brought many to this point of decision, but a person must choose whether or not he will trust Christ. I have watched people grab the seat back in front of them to control their trembling. I have seen them battle the conviction of their soul as the spiritual war rages in their heart. Nicodemus was no different. He had hung his life on his *one thing*, yet Christ was saying that his *one thing*—his religion—was the wrong thing.

Nicodemus must now decide. Will it be religion or Christ? Will he heed those words, "Ye must be born again"? What would he "do then with Jesus which is called Christ?" (Matthew 27:22). And what would he do with that *one thing*?

Nicodemus humbled himself.

Confronted with the command of Christ, Nicodemus responded with meekness. Well-trained theologians never back down from an argument, but there was no fight in this man. When Jesus informed him of his need to be born into God's family, he did not ask *why;* he asked *how.* His response was not, "Do you know who I am?" Rather, a genuinely seeking man asked a very honest question: "How can these things be?"

Perhaps pride began to rise in his heart. Perhaps Nicodemus was embarrassed by his ignorance of such an important Bible truth. Perhaps a little anger aroused in his heart at a professor who had never prepared him for this. Yet Jesus quieted any reaction with the words "Marvel not." Jesus said, "Don't be astonished or wonder at this."

Nicodemus was well on his way to making his choice. To deal with his *one thing*, he had to determine that his pride would not keep him from truth. He may have attended the classes and seminars; he may have had a degree with all the appropriate honors; he may have been so respected that he received invitations to address the multitudes. Yet that meant nothing now.

Jesus brilliantly smashed the religious pride that had blinded Nicodemus. "Art thou a master of Israel, and knowest not these things?" He had reduced the eminent Pharisee into a man who could only shake his head and admit that he could not understand. For a Pharisee to surrender any argument was an incredible step. The once proud theologian had now admitted that he didn't have all the answers; in fact, he didn't have any answers.

Jesus was attacking that *one thing*.

Truthfully, if a religious person will be born into God's family, a humbling process must take place. After investing a lifetime in a church or religion, a realization that his church has nothing to do with him going to Heaven, his gifts and offerings will never impress God, and his good works and penances do nothing to obtain eternal life, can be humiliating. How startling it must be for a religious person to open the Bible and read, "There is none righteous, no, not one… there is none that understandeth…there is none that seeketh after God…there is none that doeth good, no, not one" (Romans 3:10–12). *"No, not one!"*

There is not one Baptist good enough for Heaven! Not one Catholic good enough for Heaven! Not one Methodist good enough for Heaven! Not one Lutheran good enough for Heaven! Not one Pentecostal good enough for Heaven! Not one Jew good enough for Heaven! Not one Hindu good enough for Heaven. Not one Muslim good enough for Heaven!

Not one! Not you. Not me. Not Nicodemus.

Nicodemus examined himself.

Jesus went on to explain why Nicodemus did not have
all the answers. "Verily, verily, I say unto thee, We speak
that we do know, and testify that we have seen; and ye
receive not our witness. If I have told you earthly things,
and ye believe not, how shall ye believe, if I tell you of
heavenly things?" (John 3:11–12).

There were two sides in this struggle identified by
Christ as "we" and "ye." *We* is Jesus and His Father. *Ye*
is Nicodemus and every other religious individual who
is not born into God's family. The respected, learned
theologian of Israel was on the wrong side. And he
would never get on the right side unless he was willing
to accept the truth Christ was teaching.

Jesus told Nicodemus that before he could be
ready for a place he had never seen, he needed to accept
what Jesus was saying about a world He could see. If he
was ever going to "see" the kingdom of God, there had
to be a real life-changing birth into God's family.

Just as Nicodemus was the "ye" opposed to Christ
and His Father, we find ourselves separated from God

today. In fact, until we have been born again, the Bible refers to us as the enemies of God:

> For if, when we were enemies, we were reconciled to God by the death of his Son, much more, being reconciled, we shall be saved by his life. —ROMANS 5:10

> And you, that were sometime alienated and enemies in your mind by wicked works, yet now hath he reconciled.—COLOSSIANS 1:21

> Ye adulterers and adulteresses, know ye not that the friendship of the world is enmity with God? whosoever therefore will be a friend of the world is the enemy of God.—JAMES 4:4

Religious people point to their prayers, their gifts, their faithful church attendance, their acts of worship as proof of their piety, yet our sins alone have made us the enemies of God. It is one thing for a drunk staggering the street, a drug addict abusing his body, or an immoral deviant molesting an innocent victim to be considered an enemy of God, but for pious people like Nicodemus to be included with such scoundrels was nothing less than offensive. Yet, that is the greatest result of our sin. For all the damage our sin does to our families, our friends, and ourselves, the most detrimental consequence of our sin is its effect on our relationship with God.

I have chosen to sin. I have made myself the enemy of God. There is His side and my side. I am separated by a chasm I cannot cross on my own. I must be "born again."

No wonder it is so difficult for religious people to deal with that *one thing*! They must understand that the result of a lifetime of religious deeds and good works has done nothing but separate them from God. Those efforts have done nothing to help them get to God, but rather, they have actually made their condition worse. Swallowing religious pride can be a most distasteful thing!

Nicodemus discovered the answer.

The religious giant had crossed a barrier. When confronted with the possibility that as a master teacher he did not have all knowledge, it was normal to react with offense. Methodically, lovingly, Christ had broken his pride, and Nicodemus learned that religion, prayers, and good works could not make a man a child of God. But what was the answer?

The answer is Jesus. He reigned in Heaven as Saviour. He came to earth to be the Saviour. And He was lifted up on the cross as our Saviour. John 3:14 says, "And as Moses lifted up the serpent in the wilderness, even so must the Son of man be lifted up." When Moses lifted the serpent on the pole, it represented the sins of the Israelites. It was lifted up so all could see.

> And the LORD said unto Moses, Make thee a fiery serpent, and set it upon a pole: and it shall come to pass, that every one that is bitten, when he looketh upon it, shall live.—NUMBERS 21:8

Christ was pointing Nicodemus to the place every sinner needs to go—to the cross. When Christ died, He became "sin for us" (2 Corinthians 5:21). Like the serpent, Christ was lifted up on the cross so that not only the Romans and the Jews could see Him, but to this day, we can still see Him. As He hung between Heaven and Earth, His gruesome death displayed the ugly, sordid nature of our sins. The songwriter, Philip Bliss, elegantly stated of the cross:

> "Lifted up" was He to die,
> "It is finished!" was His cry;
> Now in Heaven exalted high:
> Hallelujah! What a Saviour![3]

And so, here was Nicodemus, duly humbled. He was no longer looking to his religion, his degrees, or his stature, but to the cross. He was ready. He was prepared for a truth so powerful, so profound, and so penetrating, the theological doctors could not comprehend it. His heart was about to be captured by a majestic, magnificent, and marvelous truth, that no book, song, or artist has ever done justice.

> *For God so loved the world, that he gave his only begotten Son, that whosoever believeth in him should not perish, but have everlasting life.*
> —JOHN 3:16

Jesus had prepared Nicodemus for the staggering words of John 3:16. This verse has been called the "gospel in a nutshell." It has been the theme of countless sermons and songs, and it is one of the first verses many children will learn in Sunday school. It is a verse of great simplicity, yet it was spoken to an astute doctor of religion!

No wonder Jesus said, "Whosoever shall not receive the kingdom of God as a little child shall in no wise enter therein" (Luke 18:17). Profound Bible truth is not reserved for the seminary professor, for Jesus has "hid these things from the wise and prudent, and hast revealed them unto babes" (Matthew 11:25). Repeatedly, Jesus reminded His disciples to "suffer little children to come unto me, and forbid them not: for of such is the kingdom of God" (Luke 18:16).

Little ones do not have the veneer of complicated religious teaching clouding their understanding of Christ and salvation. They do not understand the religious hierarchy that limits truth to a select few. They are not intimidated by master teachers and the like. They understand simplicity.

What John 3:16 can do…

It was a bitter, cold day in a Midwestern city where a poor boy shivered on a street corner selling newspapers. The swirling wind seemed to blow the snow in every direction, and there were very few customers buying papers. His threadbare coat coupled with his tattered clothes and worn shoes made him an object of pity.

A policeman happened by and told the boy to go home. It was too cold and too dangerous to be outside. He responded, "Sir, I have no home. I sleep in alleys and parks. Do you know anyone who would want me?"

The officer said, "Come with me." He took his hand and led him a few blocks away. Pointing to a large, brick house, he told the boy, "Go up and knock on that door. When the lady comes, say to her, 'John 3:16,' and she will let you in."

"What does that mean?"

"You don't need to worry about it. All you need to do is knock on the door and say, 'John 3:16.'"

The boy made his way up the concrete steps rehearsing those words. "John 3:16. John 3:16." He tapped on the door until a kind lady answered. The little fellow looked up at the tender woman and said, "John 3:16."

"Well, why didn't you say so! Come right in!" She took his frayed coat, ushering him into a large sitting room where a roaring fire filled the fireplace. She told him to get comfortable while she prepared something for him to eat. As the fire melted his nearly frozen limbs, he thought to himself, "I don't know what this John 3:16 thing means, but it sure can make a cold boy warm!"

The meal was quickly prepared. As the boy sat at the table eating, he couldn't remember the last time his little stomach was filled. He ate until he could eat no more, and then thought, "I don't understand what John 3:16 is, but it sure can make a hungry boy full!"

The gracious woman led him to a warm bath. As he scrubbed himself, letting the waters thaw his body, he thought, "I sure don't understand what John 3:16 is, but it sure can make a dirty boy clean!"

She returned with new pajamas. Soon he was tucked into a toasty bed with crisp sheets and a new blanket. As the little guy fell asleep, the last thing he thought was, "I still don't get this John 3:16, but it sure can give a tired boy rest!"

Early the next morning, he awoke to the smell of breakfast being prepared. He dressed and went to find the wonderful lady who had been so kind to him. With trusting eyes, he looked up and asked her, "Ma'am, can you tell me what John 3:16 means?" She brought him into the sitting room and opened her Bible to those wonderful words. She explained how God loved him so much that He gave His son to die for him. Then she shared with him that wonderful promise, "that whosoever believeth in him should not perish, but have everlasting life."

Soon the young boy was on his knees, calling on the name of Christ and trusting Him to take his sins away. While this young boy may not have understood all of John 3:16, the simple truth of this verse had captivated his heart and led to him with childlike faith to trust Christ as his Saviour.

Yes, the truth of John 3:16 can indeed make a cold heart warm, an empty life full, a dirty soul clean, and a tired heart rested. All because Jesus paid for our sins.

———————

How simple is the gospel? Throughout Scripture God reveals it to us.

And they said, Believe on the Lord Jesus Christ, and thou shalt be saved, and thy house.—ACTS 16:31

For whosoever shall call upon the name of the Lord shall be saved.—ROMANS 10:13

But as many as received him, to them gave he power to become the sons of God, even to them that believe on his name.—JOHN 1:12

He that hath the Son hath life; and he that hath not the Son of God hath not life.—1 JOHN 5:12

It doesn't take a degree, a religion, or a teacher to understand these verses, but it does take faith. And while many religious people are convinced there is some impressive work they must do to earn God's favor, a little child is far more inclined to see in John 3:16 what the religious slave cannot.

God loves me! God loves me so much He gave His Son to die for me. He wants me to have eternal life. I can choose to believe on Him. He promised that I would not perish but have everlasting life.

How simple if you are a child. How complicated if your *one thing* is religion.

So, Nicodemus, what does John 3:16 mean to you? Perhaps he thought, "I sure don't understand it all. I can't fathom why God would love me so much that He would give His Son to die on the cross for me. I don't understand why He would be willing to receive me into His family. I can't figure out what I have that He would want. But this *one thing* I do know! John 3:16 can take a man chained by the bondage of religion and set him free! John 3:16 can take a man plagued by the fear of man and replace that fear with the love of God. John 3:16 can take an old, lost Pharisee, and save him for all eternity!"

The powerful words of this simple truth brought a confused, arrogant, religious man to a point of humility, decision, and belief. It was his answer. And it is the answer to your *one thing*.

Chapter Two

A WOMAN OF SAMARIA

Immersed in Sin

W e "must needs go through Samaria." Those words caused an internal groan among Christ's disciples in John 4. The Pharisees had discovered that Jesus was baptizing more disciples than John, so a journey from Judaea to the Sea of Galilee was in order. The disciples were unaware of the impeccable timing of the Son of God.

Notice what the Bible says in John 4:

When therefore the Lord knew how the Pharisees had heard that Jesus made and baptized more

*disciples than John, (Though Jesus himself baptized
not, but his disciples,) He left Judæa, and departed
again into Galilee. And he must needs go through
Samaria...Now Jacob's well was there. Jesus
therefore, being wearied with his journey, sat thus
on the well: and it was about the sixth hour. There
cometh a woman of Samaria to draw water: Jesus
saith unto her, Give me to drink. (For his disciples
were gone away unto the city to buy meat.) Then
saith the woman of Samaria unto him, How is it
that thou, being a Jew, askest drink of me, which
am a woman of Samaria? for the Jews have no
dealings with the Samaritans. Jesus answered
and said unto her, If thou knewest the gift of God,
and who it is that saith to thee, Give me to drink;
thou wouldest have asked of him, and he would
have given thee living water. The woman saith
unto him, Sir, thou hast nothing to draw with,
and the well is deep: from whence then hast thou
that living water?...Jesus answered and said unto
her, Whosoever drinketh of this water shall thirst
again: But whosoever drinketh of the water that
I shall give him shall never thirst; but the water
that I shall give him shall be in him a well of water
springing up into everlasting life. The woman*

saith unto him, Sir, give me this water, that I thirst not, neither come hither to draw. Jesus saith unto her, Go, call thy husband, and come hither. The woman answered and said, I have no husband. Jesus said unto her, Thou hast well said, I have no husband: For thou hast had five husbands; and he whom thou now hast is not thy husband: in that saidst thou truly. The woman saith unto him, Sir, I perceive that thou art a prophet. Our fathers worshipped in this mountain; and ye say, that in Jerusalem is the place where men ought to worship. Jesus saith unto her, Woman, believe me, the hour cometh, when ye shall neither in this mountain, nor yet at Jerusalem, worship the Father. Ye worship ye know not what: we know what we worship: for salvation is of the Jews. But the hour cometh, and now is, when the true worshippers shall worship the Father in spirit and in truth: for the Father seeketh such to worship him. God is a Spirit: and they that worship him must worship him in spirit and in truth. The woman saith unto him, I know that Messias cometh, which is called Christ: when he is come, he will tell us all things. Jesus saith unto her, I that speak unto thee am he.

...The woman then left her waterpot, and went her way into the city, and saith to the men, Come, see a man, which told me all things that ever I did: is not this the Christ?—JOHN 9:1–3, 6–17, 24–25, 33–38

Such an excursion would take three days, and it presented two choices—a trip to the east along the Jordan River, or a slightly more direct path that led through the land of Samaria. Either route presented a conundrum for the Jews of the first century. The eastern route almost certainly meant interaction with Gentiles, yet a trip through Samaria meant contact with Samaritans. Neither thought was pleasant to the prejudiced mind of that day, but as distasteful as the Gentiles were, the animosity toward the Samaritans was even deeper. Centuries earlier invading Assyrians had married Jews creating a "half-breed," resulting in lasting resentment and hatred. Their grudge was now going on 750 years.

It was usually agreed that the lesser of two evils was the meeting with a Gentile, so the more frequently chosen itinerary was the eastern path. On this occasion, however, Jesus made it clear that they *must* take the Samaritan route. There was a critical reason for this decision.

A woman lived in Samaria. And there was *one thing* in her life Christ needed to confront.

Jesus and His disciples were roughly halfway on their trip to Galilee when they came to a city called Sychar, and a very holy, revered place known as Jacob's well. The actual locations of many sacred sites in the Holy Land are debated, but not this one. Four hundred yards to the north lay the tomb of Joseph, with the religious center of Mount Gerizim standing tall in the background. What a perfect background for a woman to deal with her *one thing*.

The road to Sychar was some forty miles, and the entourage arrived at noon ready for lunch. While the disciples were procuring food, Jesus was interested in a meat they knew not of. More important than eating food was doing the will of His Father and finishing His work. Doing His Father's work meant that Jesus needed to confront a Samaritan woman with her sin.

Jacob's well is covered by a capstone twenty inches thick and some five feet across. As Jesus was sitting on the well, the woman came to draw water. As a Jew it was unthinkable that Jesus would ever speak with a Samaritan. As a male Jew, it was more unfathomable that He would speak publicly with any woman. The Jewish rabbis wanted women to stay "in their place," a place where husbands avoided even speaking with their wives in public, let alone a stranger. To make matters worse, Jesus was about to engage the woman in a theological discussion—this was unheard of![4]

But the norms of first-century religion and the purpose of the Son of God were very different. From the moment His mother was "found with child of the Holy Ghost" (Matthew 1:18), until He ascended into Heaven, it was apparent that Jesus and the religious establishment were on a collision course. If His disciples would ever be prepared to go to "all nations" (Matthew 28:19) and to preach to "every creature" (Mark 16:15), there had to be repeated encounters with Samaritans and Canaanites and other assorted nationalities. Racial and religious prejudices had to be set aside.

Jesus was just getting started. He said to the woman, "Give me to drink." Not only did He speak with her, He was humble enough to ask for her help and was willing to even drink from her cup. To the religious ruling class, the cup of that Samaritan woman was as unclean and defiled as any vessel could possibly be, yet the Creator of the wells, brooks, rivers, and seas was asking her for water.

The woman responded with a quick mind and a sharp tongue. She immediately dredged up centuries of battles and feuds with the reminder that the Jews "have no dealings with the Samaritans" (John 4:9). Prejudiced people rarely admit that they live just as their hated foes do, for she well could have added that the Samaritans had no dealings with the Jews. But Jesus refused to take the bait. Instead of pouring gas on the fire, Jesus presented her the offer of a lifetime: "If thou knewest the gift of God, and who it is that saith to thee, Give me to drink; thou wouldest have asked of him, and he would have given thee living water" (John 4:10).

In one simple sentence, He told her everything she needed to know in order to be saved. Eternal life is available. It is a free gift—Jesus gives it. All you must do is ask!

Sometimes we make so complicated what Jesus made so simple! We have analyses and explanations and sermons that carry on interminably. But Jesus said it all in a few phrases that most likely took no more than ten seconds to quote. Jesus told her to forget the religious debates. He reminded her that what mattered was her eternity, and the only hope for her soul was the living water of God.

Instead of fighting for nationalism and patriotism and "who is better," Jesus compassionately offered the greatest gift a person can receive, and His gentle, gracious spirit disarmed her. Her words of disdain and perhaps even disgust in verse 9, were quickly replaced by a very respectable "sir" in verse 11. She wanted to win the argument, but Jesus wanted to win her soul.

He continued: "Whosoever drinketh of this water shall thirst again: But whosoever drinketh of the water that I shall give him shall never thirst; but the water that I shall give him shall be in him a well of water springing up into everlasting life" (John 4:13–14).

Word by word, line by line—like a judicious lawyer—Jesus explained Bible salvation. He pleaded with her to consider eternity, inviting her to freely drink from the well of everlasting life. It was an offer too good to refuse, so she said, "give me this water, that I thirst not, neither come hither to draw." Like so many today, she had confused her temporal need and her eternal need. Many people want a religion that will fix their present issues, but they never consider the permanent problem that exists within them. "*Fix* me" is not the same as "*Save* me."

Had Jesus considered her a number to put on a scoreboard, He might have led her in what is known as a "sinner's prayer" and been done with it. He could have added another act of religion to her resume, but that prayer would not have saved her soul. Prayers do not save. Jesus saves.

And if that woman was to be saved, there was another thing they must deal with. It was her *one thing*.

Sin or Saviour?

Jesus saith unto her, Go, call thy husband, and come hither.—JOHN 4:16

Multitudes of classes and sermons have instructed God's people on methods and strategies of bringing a lost sinner to the Saviour. The most famous of these plans is a simple walk through a number of Scriptures called the Romans Road. Some will use the Isaiah 53 plan. Others might prefer John 3. But very few Christians have been known to use the "go call thy husband" plan. But that is exactly what Jesus said to this woman.

The words of Jesus seem to fly in the face of logical thinking. After all, the woman claimed she wanted the living water. Jesus said she simply needed to ask. Why not close the deal? The last thing a preacher ever wants to do with a soul in the balance is to change the subject. Often, as the Bible is opened and a sinner has come to the realization that Christ is the Saviour, Satan finds a way to bring a distraction— the baby cries, the phone rings, or the kids argue. He is the master of changing the dialogue.

But in this story, Jesus is the one changing the direction of the conversation. She responded by informing Him that she had "no husband." Technically, she was telling the truth, but, as one writer so astutely put it, she forgot to add the word *presently*.[5] Jewish tradition permitted a woman to be married three times over the course of a lifetime, but she had long since passed that standard.[6] She had been married five times and was now living in an adulterous relationship.

What powerful, convicting words came from the Son of God! "Thou hast well said, I have no husband: For thou hast had five husbands; and he whom thou now hast is not thy husband: in that saidst thou truly" (John 4:17).

Jesus did not avoid the issue; He met it head on. He did not soften His words. He was blunt, clear, and inflexible. The woman was living in immorality, and Jesus called out her sin.

In the United States, there are 7.5 million couples living in adultery, a number that has doubled in the past ten years.[7] One doctor touts the great advantage to cohabitation, in that instead of 'til death do you part, relationships are now a one-year lease.[8] Forbes.com advises that "living together makes more sense than marriage,"[9] and even some ministers refuse to take a stand, lest they make anyone feel uncomfortable or judged.

Perhaps the reason America is drowning in adultery reverts to the pulpits, where ministers refuse to preach as Jesus preached. Jesus was not worried whether or not the woman was feeling comfortable, nor was He concerned that she might feel as if she were being judged. Jesus was not trying to get the woman to like Him.

He was trying to save her.

And if she was going to be saved, she had to deal with this *one thing*: "Do I want my sin, or do I want the Saviour to wash my sin away?"

It is critically important to understand that the woman of Samaria would never go to Heaven by quitting her adultery, or for that matter, any other sin. The Bible is not just clear on this matter, it is profusely clear.

Not by works of righteousness which we have done, but according to his mercy he saved us, by the washing of regeneration, and renewing of the Holy Ghost.—TITUS 3:5

Therefore by the deeds of the law there shall no flesh be justified in his sight: for by the law is the knowledge of sin.—ROMANS 3:20

Therefore we conclude that a man is justified by faith without the deeds of the law.—ROMANS 3:28

But to him that worketh not, but believeth on him that justifieth the ungodly, his faith is counted for righteousness.—ROMANS 4:5

And if by grace, then is it no more of works: otherwise grace is no more grace. But if it be of works, then is it no more grace: otherwise work is no more work.—ROMANS 11:6

Knowing that a man is not justified by the works of the law, but by the faith of Jesus Christ, even

*we have believed in Jesus Christ, that we might be
justified by the faith of Christ, and not by the works
of the law: for by the works of the law shall no flesh
be justified.*—GALATIANS 2:16

*Who hath saved us, and called us with an holy
calling, not according to our works, but according
to his own purpose and grace, which was
given us in Christ Jesus before the world began.*
—2 TIMOTHY 1:9

Yet, there was still a decision to be made.
When Christ saves a person, He cleanses us from
"all unrighteousness" (1 John 1:9). He redeems
us from "all iniquity" (Titus 2:14), and we are
"justified" (Romans 5:9). Because He bore the "sins
of many" (Hebrews 9:28), He is able to "put away
sin" (Hebrews 9:26) and remember them "no
more" (Hebrews 8:12). These verses join countless
other promises in the Bible describing the wonder
of God's gracious forgiveness, yet that forgiveness
is never forced on an individual. A question has to
be considered: "Do I want my sin; or do I want the
Saviour to wash away my sin?"

Lust dominated the life of this woman, yet Jesus was offering complete forgiveness. She had to decide if she wanted that forgiveness.

For many, the *one thing* that keeps them from Christ is a controlling sin. It may be the sin of drunkenness, immorality, drug abuse, covetousness, pride, selfishness, or jealousy. It may be a sin that is written across the walls of their lives for all to see, or it may be covertly hidden in the depths of their hearts. Regardless of the sin, its consequences cannot be avoided.

Ask yourself this question: Will I allow this *one thing* to keep me from trusting Christ as my Saviour?

The Samaritan woman argued religion.

How uncomfortable the woman of Samaria must have been! Jesus was no longer a "sir," He was now a "prophet," and with the weight of conviction bearing on her soul, she resorted to a religious debate. "Our fathers worshipped in this mountain; and ye say, that in Jerusalem is the place where men ought to worship"

(John 4:20). How classic! "Let's argue religion!" And what an argument it was!

Centuries earlier, the Samaritans offered to assist the Jews in their rebuilding of the temple in Jerusalem. When that overture was rejected, the offended Samaritans decided to build their own rival temple as if to say, "You worship in your temple on Mount Moriah. We worship in our temple on Mount Gerizim."

She might have added, "Abraham, Jacob, Joseph, and Joshua visited our mountain. Our mountain was a city of refuge. Our mountain is the great mountain where God taught His people when they entered the Promised Land!" She might have repeated the legends the Samaritans were teaching about Mount Gerizim, "Our mountain was the place of the Garden of Eden. Adam was made from the dust of our mountain. Noah's ark landed at our mountain. Abraham offered his son on our mountain. And everybody knows that Jacob's ladder went from Heaven to our mountain."[10]

When tourists visit the Holy Land they are bombarded with sites. There are many that are accurate and many more that are presumed, but religious pilgrims want to touch and feel and experience. It is the nature of religion to emphasize places, but with Christ, the emphasis is on a person.

> *Jesus saith unto her, Woman, believe me, the hour cometh, when ye shall neither in this mountain, nor yet at Jerusalem, worship the Father. Ye worship ye know not what: we know what we worship: for salvation is of the Jews. But the hour cometh, and now is, when the true worshippers shall worship the Father in spirit and in truth: for the Father seeketh such to worship him.*—JOHN 4:21–23

Religion points to holy places, temples, statues, and mountains, but God does not look to those things. He does not want us to make a pilgrimage or erect a shrine. He does not want us to glorify an abbey, a basilica, a cathedral, a chapel, a church, a parish, a sacellum, a sanctuary, a tabernacle, or a temple. You don't need a Mecca, a River Ganges, a Jerusalem, a Vatican, or even a Salt Lake City!

"God is a Spirit," thus He seeks those who will "worship him in spirit and in truth" (John 4:24). If a sinner like the woman of Samaria—or like me or you—will ever be forgiven, it is because we do not look to religion, we look to *truth*. So the question is simple: What is truth?

"Sanctify them through thy truth: thy word is truth" (John 17:17). Jesus said, "Search the scriptures; for in them ye think ye have eternal life: and they are they which testify of me" (John 5:39). If you want to go to Heaven, go to the Bible. Jesus didn't say to go to a shrine. He said to go to His Word!

The true Christ is revealed.

The woman saith unto him, I know that Messias cometh, which is called Christ: when he is come, he will tell us all things.—JOHN 4:25

The Samaritan woman was beginning to grasp the truth. Forget your mountains. Forget your legends. Forget your notions. You need the Messiah. You need Christ. You need the anointed Son of God to wash your sins permanently away. You don't need a religion. You need a Saviour! And that Saviour is the Lord Jesus

Christ. He simply said, "I that speak unto thee am he" (John 4:26).

Woven throughout the book of John is the wonderful title for the Lord Jesus Christ "I am." He is the great "I am."

I am the bread of life.—JOHN 6:35

I am the living bread which came down from heaven.—JOHN 6:51

I am from him, and he hath sent me.—JOHN 7:29

I am the light of the world.—JOHN 8:12

I am from above.—JOHN 8:23

Verily, verily, I say unto you, Before Abraham was, I am.—JOHN 8:58

I am the door of the sheep.—JOHN 10:7

I am the door: by me if any man enter in, he shall be saved, and shall go in and out, and find pasture.—JOHN 10:9

I am the good shepherd.—JOHN 10:11

I am the resurrection, and the life.—JOHN 11:25

Ye call me Master and Lord: and ye say well; for so
I am.—JOHN 13:13

I am the way, the truth, and the life.—JOHN 14:6

I am the true vine.—JOHN 15:1

It is stated so succinctly yet so perfectly in Exodus 3:14. He is the *"I AM THAT I AM."*

In these days of confusion we cry out, "Who is the Saviour?" Jesus simply responds, "I am." We ask, "Who is the one who can take my sins and guilt away?" Jesus answers, "I am." Our soul wonders, "Who is the one who can take me to Heaven?" The simple reply from Jesus is, "I am." He is not a part of salvation. He is not an integral ingredient of salvation. He is not a critical component of salvation.

He *is* salvation!

A pastor and songwriter wrote it like this a century ago:

> Jesus Christ is made to me,
> All I need, all I need.

He alone is all my plea,
He is all I need.

Wisdom, righteousness, and power,
Holiness forevermore.
My redemption full and free,
He is all I need.[11]

The Samaritan woman knew that the Messiah was coming, and when Jesus revealed that He was the Christ, she was amazed. She left her waterpot behind, went back into the city, and said, "Come, see a man, which told me all things that ever I did: is not this the Christ?" (John 4:29). She had made her choice: "I want a Saviour to wash my sins away." Her life was changed! Her sins were gone!

Her *one thing* was conquered.

Her *one thing* was forgiven.

Do you want His forgiveness, His cleansing, His peace? Then you must make a choice: Do you want your sin, or do you want the Saviour to wash your sin away?

What is that *one thing* that is keeping you from Christ?

The power of Christ is greater than the power of any "one thing."

In the late 1930s, thousands had assembled at the famed Billy Sunday Tabernacle in Winona Lake, Indiana. The featured speaker, Mel Trotter, had recently returned to the United States, having preached revival meetings in the British Isles, and the audience came expecting to hear glorious reports from those meetings. As he perused the crowd, the preacher was moved by the number of young people in attendance, and when he stood to address them, he was impressed of God to give his testimony.

Mel's father was a bartender who drank as much as he served while his mother stayed home and prayed for their family. The two divergent lifestyles forced a young teenager to choose a path to walk, and sadly he chose to follow his father. By the age of nineteen, liquor controlled young Mel to the extent he could not keep a job. He and his new wife moved to a rural community in Iowa, but the habit followed him there. For all of his efforts, he could not quit his sin.

A newborn baby gave Mel a fresh desire to put the bottle away, but it wasn't long before he was drinking worse than before. It was the *one thing* ruining his life and marriage.

The bouts with booze increased, and it wasn't uncommon for Mel to leave his family for days at a time. He was miserable, yet it seemed that there was nothing he could do to stop.

After a ten-day drinking binge, Mel returned home to find his wife holding their dead child. Convinced it was his drinking that had murdered his child, he promised his wife that he would never touch liquor again, yet, two hours after the funeral, he was so drunk he could barely stagger home.

Disgusted, Mel Trotter decided to run. He hopped a freight train headed to Chicago, and on January 19, 1897, the train rolled into the city during a blinding snowstorm. Penniless, he sold his shoes to buy one more drink. When that money was gone, the saloonkeeper kicked him into the streets.

A broken, despondent man looked at his wasted, empty life and convinced himself there was nothing worth saving. "Perhaps, I should end it all." Mel made his way toward Lake Michigan where he planned to take his life.

Suddenly, Mel felt a hand on his shoulder. A former jockey and card shark, Tom Mackey, was inviting him to step inside a building called the Pacific Garden Mission. Trotter staggered in just in time to hear the director of the mission, Harry Monroe, share his own story. At the age of twenty-seven his life had been transformed by the power of Christ.

There was hope for Mel. "If God could save that twenty-seven-year-old drunk, God could save this twenty-seven-year-old drunk," he thought. That night, a broken man bowed his knee to Christ and was wonderfully saved.

Mel Trotter would discover that any man trusting Christ became a "new creature." The old life "passed away," and everything became new (2 Corinthians 5:17). God had saved his soul, and in time, changed his life, took away the booze, restored his marriage, called him to be a preacher, and used him to spend his life rescuing helpless sinners on the streets. His story was a wonderful testimony of the power of God to change a life.[12]

When Mel finished telling his story, a preacher named Harry Rimmer remarked that everything changes when Jesus comes. The phrase stuck in the mind of a noted songwriter named Homer Rodeheaver, and with the help of another pastor, he penned these words:

> *So men today have found the Saviour able,*
> *They could not conquer passion, lust, and sin;*
> *Their broken hearts had left them sad and lonely,*
> *Then Jesus came and dwelt Himself within.*
>
> *When Jesus comes the tempter's power is broken;*
> *When Jesus comes the tears are wiped away.*
> *He takes the gloom and fills the life with glory,*
> *For all is changed when Jesus comes to stay.*[13]

Countless individuals could join the woman of Samaria and Mel Trotter in describing a life changed by the power of Christ. He has the power to wash the darkest sin away, and He has the power to make all things new.

He has the power over that *one thing*.

Chapter Three

A BLIND MAN
Needing Spiritual Healing

I n John 9, the Bible tells us that there was a blind man who needed spiritual healing in his life.

And as Jesus passed by, he saw a man which was blind from his birth. And his disciples asked him, saying, Master, who did sin, this man, or his parents, that he was born blind? Jesus answered, Neither hath this man sinned, nor his parents: but that the works of God should be made manifest in him...When he had thus spoken, he spat on the ground, and made clay of the spittle, and he anointed the eyes of the blind man with the clay, And said unto him, Go, wash in the pool of Siloam…He went his way therefore, and washed, and came seeing.

The neighbours therefore, and they which before had seen him that he was blind, said, Is not this he that sat and begged? Some said, This is he: others said, He is like him: but he said, I am he. Therefore said they unto him, How were thine eyes opened? He answered and said, A man that is called Jesus made clay, and anointed mine eyes, and said unto me, Go to the pool of Siloam, and wash: and I went and washed, and I received sight. Then said they unto him, Where is he? He said, I know not.

They brought to the Pharisees him that aforetime was blind. And it was the sabbath day when Jesus made the clay, and opened his eyes. Then again the Pharisees also asked him how he had received his sight. He said unto them, He put clay upon mine eyes, and I washed, and do see. Therefore said some of the Pharisees, This man is not of God, because he keepeth not the sabbath day. Others said, How can a man that is a sinner do such miracles? And there was a division among them. They say unto the blind man again, What sayest thou of him, that he hath opened thine

eyes? He said, He is a prophet...Then again called
they the man that was blind, and said unto him,
Give God the praise: we know that this man is a
sinner. He answered and said, Whether he be a
sinner or no, I know not: one thing I know, that,
whereas I was blind, now I see...They answered
and said unto him, Thou wast altogether born in
sins, and dost thou teach us? And they cast him
out. Jesus heard that they had cast him out; and
when he had found him, he said unto him, Dost
thou believe on the Son of God? He answered
and said, Who is he, Lord, that I might believe
on him? And Jesus said unto him, Thou hast both
seen him, and it is he that talketh with thee. And
he said, Lord, I believe. And he worshipped him.
—JOHN 9:1–3, 6–17, 24–25, 33–38

One of the most common questions thrown
back at preachers is, "Why does God allow so much
suffering? If God loves people, why doesn't He
intervene?" We have an insatiable desire to understand
the reason for so much pain.

But the truth is that people rarely flip the
question inside out. We don't usually look at someone

with the blessing of God in their life and wonder why God permits such happiness, or stop to think that the everyday goodness of our personal lives is from Him. If an NFL quarterback should ever stoop to praise God for the ability to play a game, the reaction from the media establishment usually would be abject horror. We tend to take credit for the good and find a way to assign blame for the bad. Often, that blame is pointed at God.

Perhaps that is the reason for the question of the disciples in John 9:2, "Master, who did sin, this man, or his parents, that he was born blind?" It was very clear to them that someone was guilty here, and they were simply asserting the long-standing belief taught by the religious leaders of their day that if a person was blind, deaf, or lame, it was a consequence of sin. That condition was normally blamed on the parents, but some sages believed that it was possible for a baby to sin while still in the mother's womb. Such a defiled infant would have to pay for his sin the rest of his life.[14]

There is another human tendency found in this question. The disciples are giving the Creator of the Universe two choices—either this man sinned or his parents sinned. Evidently, the thought did not enter their minds that the correct answer may be something they had not considered. God's Word says, "My thoughts are not your thoughts, Neither are your ways my ways, saith the Lord" (Isaiah 55:8), and issuing a multiple choice question to the Lord was probably not too wise.

Jesus responded by informing His disciples that there was a reason for the blindness that transcended their thinking. Their religion and preconceptions did not allow them to envisage the possibility that a person's malady could exist because of the love of God. Yet, that is why the man was blind. It was not his parent's sin. It was not his own sin. He was blind so that the "works of God should be made manifest in him" (John 9:3). If he were not blind, he could never have experienced the vast mercy and grace of God. Blindness was not his greatest curse; it turned out to be his greatest blessing.

It was his blindness that allowed Jesus to deal with his *one thing.*

Notice again the statement of Christ. He wanted
to do "works" (emphasis on the plural) in his life.
The first work was an obvious one. Jesus "spat on the
ground, and made clay of the spittle, and he anointed
the eyes of the blind man with the clay, and said unto
him, 'Go, wash in the pool of Siloam,' (which is by
interpretation, Sent.) He went his way therefore, and
washed, and came seeing" (John 9:7).

What a mighty work! Jesus opened the man's eyes
proving His claim to be the Son of God. The man's
neighbors were stunned and confused; the religious
establishment was befuddled; and even his parents
had no answer. Once again, humans and their refusal
to trust God had created a perplexity only faith
could explain.

But the story had just begun. Though Jesus was
concerned about the man's physical sight, He was far
more interested in his spiritual sight. He wanted to
open the eyes of his soul. Jesus would inform them
and us that it was for "judgment I am come into this
world" (John 9:39), and unless the scales were removed
from the eyes of their souls, they would be lost for

eternity. The biggest problem in this man's life was not his *physical* blindness; it was his *spiritual* blindness.

It was his *one thing*.

Suppose this gentleman could find his way through time and eternity and speak with us today. Certainly, his testimony would sound something like this:

"If you were to ask me 1,980 years ago about the greatest event in my life, I would have told you of the day Christ opened my eyes. What a day it was! Jesus spat upon the ground, turned the spittle into clay, rubbed it over my eyes, and told me to go and wash in the pool of Siloam.

"That fifteen minute walk seemed to take forever! I never experienced such hope, yet a part of me was convinced it was too good to be true. But sure enough, when I washed in the Siloam pool, I could instantly see! I will never forget the overwhelming flood of colors, the delicate petals of a flower, the majestic mountains of Jerusalem, and the charming face of a child. In that split second of time my life was forever changed. Jesus healed me! I would never in a million years know such a grand experience in my life.

"Or so I thought. Eternity has taught me a different lesson. Something happened that day far more wonderful than Jesus opening my physical eyes. I saw Jesus the Saviour—not just the miracle worker, not just the gracious, kind, compassionate minister. I saw Him as the anointed Saviour of Israel. I saw Him as the one who had not only the power, but also the yearning to take my sins away. I saw Him as my personal Saviour.

"The greatest moment of my life was that instant my spiritual eyes were opened. The cataracts on the eyes of my heart were removed, and standing in front of me was the hope of my soul. I said, 'Lord, I believe!' That was all. I simply believed that Jesus is the Son of God. I simply believed that He is the only one who can take my sins away. I simply believed that He is my only Saviour.

"'*Lord, I believe!*' He did all the rest! Earlier He washed my blindness away. Now He washed my sins away. Years later I can boldly testify that Jesus did a wonderful thing for me when He washed all my sins away!"

As human beings, we marvel at the mighty *work* Jesus did, yet remember, Jesus wants to do *works*. We often settle for the temporary, but Jesus is the master of the permanent. It is not enough to cure a man's physical blindness when his real problem is his spiritual blindness.

It is that *one thing*.

Comparatively, it was far easier for Christ to give the man a new set of eyes than it was to give him a new heart. He simply allowed Jesus to make the clay, apply the clay, and then obeyed the command to wash the clay away, and in so doing, he was healed. But the matter of his spiritual blindness was a far more complex issue, so Jesus got to work. To help overcome his *one thing*, there were four lessons Jesus had to teach him.

He had to learn that religion is not the answer.

There were at least eight other occasions in the New Testament where Jesus healed blind people, and in each case, the healing was instantaneous. Sometimes Jesus touched the person. Other times He simply spoke, but in each instance the miracle was immediate. The very fact that Jesus made the clay, anointed his eyes, and sent him on the journey should arrest our attention. Jesus wanted to do *works* in the man's life, the greatest of which was the saving of his soul.

In the account, the timing of the miracle takes center stage. "It was the sabbath day when Jesus made the clay, and opened his eyes" (John 9:14). That fact became the point of argument among the religious community. "Therefore said some of the Pharisees, This man is not of God, because he keepeth not the sabbath day. Others said, How can a man that is a sinner do such miracles? And there was a division among them" (John 9:16). And we see in the same verse that, of course, there "was a division among them."

A sect known as the Pharisees controlled religious Israel in the time of Christ. These deeply pious individuals had their foundations in the Old Testament, with origins tied to the sacred study of the Scriptures. As their influence grew, they were impressed to comment on the 613 laws of God, and soon their oral rules and traditions were studied along with the Bible.

It didn't take very long for religion to do what it always does. The bigger the religion, the less room there is for the Bible. By the time Jesus was walking the sands of Israel, religious rules and orders had superseded the Bible. Human beings had created rules to cover every known aspect of life, and when they were finished doing that, they proceeded to write rules to cover the rules.

Religious rulebooks have a way of making the United States Tax Code look like a second-grade reader. The Jews had rules for everything. There were rules on how to have clean pots, clean pans, clean tents, clean clothes, clean utensils, and clean hands, but not clean hearts. Though there were plenty of rules for everyday life, the Sabbath was the day the religious rulebook was created for.

The Lord touched on the Sabbath in only a few phrases: "But the seventh day is the sabbath of the

Lord thy God: in it thou shalt not do any work, thou, nor thy son, nor thy daughter, thy manservant, nor thy maidservant, nor thy cattle, nor thy stranger that is within thy gates: For in six days the Lord made heaven and earth, the sea, and all that in them is, and rested the seventh day: wherefore the Lord blessed the sabbath day, and hallowed it" (Exodus 20:10–11).

But the Jews *majored* on the Sabbath day.

When the oral religious rulebook was finally written down, it had some two million words. Some of the Sabbath restrictions went like this:

"A woman may not go out with bands of wool or bands of flax...she might not go outdoors with a hair net, nor with a necklace or nose rings...or with a needle which has no eye."

"A man...might not go out with sandals shod with nails. A woman might not leave the house with a spice box or a perfume flask."

Many of the sages forbad a woman to go to a "public place with a false tooth" on the Sabbath. "If a man's teeth pain him he may not suck vinegar through them on the Sabbath."

If someone died on the Sabbath, it was forbidden to close his eyes. The good news, however, was that a father was allowed to deliver a baby if his wife went into labor on the Sabbath and to "tie up the navel string."

They had to count the number of steps they would take on the Sabbath. They had to be careful where they fell asleep on the Sabbath. Children learned the Sabbath rules before they could add or subtract.[15]

Solomon once said, "Of making many books there is no end" (Ecclesiastes 2:12). When it came to making many rules, the Pharisees never got around to "The End."

The fact that Jesus had spat on the ground, mixed the dirt and saliva, and then produced the clay, was a clear violation of the rulebook (though it in no way violated the Bible). "The act of kneading (which is involved in making mud from saliva and dirt) was regarded as one of the thirty-nine forms of work that violated the Sabbath."[16] Even though it would be grudgingly admitted the cause was good, the majority of the religious establishment could not get over the fact that this Jesus had worked on the Sabbath.

But Jesus was dealing with our friend's *one thing*. His spiritual eyes could not be opened until he saw that all the righteous works, all the religious rules, and all the refined actions that human beings attempt in their desire to impress God are not only useless, they are in fact hurtful.

> *But we are all as an unclean thing, and all our righteousnesses are as filthy rags.*—ISAIAH 64:6

> *When I shall say to the righteous, that he shall surely live; if he trust to his own righteousness, and commit iniquity, all his righteousnesses shall not be remembered; but for his iniquity that he hath committed, he shall die for it.*—EZEKIEL 33:13

> *Now to him that worketh is the reward not reckoned of grace, but of debt.*—ROMANS 4:4

How religion blinds! All of our self-righteous acts, our prayers, our gifts, our confessions, do not help us get to God. They actually make things worse. We convince ourselves that God must be impressed by our actions, that He must accept our sacrifices; yet the more we work at salvation, the greater the debt becomes! Before spiritually blinded eyes can be opened, a person must see that God is not looking for religion.

The blind man had to learn that prophets are not the answer.

When ushered before the councils of the Pharisees, the cured man was asked his opinion on the healer of his eyes. He did not hesitate, "He is a prophet."

Wrong answer.

The illustrious history of Israel had produced many mighty prophets, but none had the power to save. From the determined faith of Abraham, to the legendary leadership of Moses, to the glorious singing of David, to the mighty thundering of Elijah, to the precious promises of Isaiah, to the fascinating prophecies of Daniel, the history of the Jews boasted preachers like no other nation. Their biographies were captivating, their preaching convicting, yet not one of them could save a soul. Not one dared to have the audacity of claiming to do what only God can do—forgive sins. The Jews knew this. On another occasion, they put forth the rhetorical question, "Who can forgive sins, but God alone?" (Luke 5:21).

These well-known prophets had come; they had ministered; they had died, and with a new set of eyes, the blind man could visit and see many of their tombs. They had served faithfully and they had served well—some even giving their lives—but none of them could save a poor blind man 1,980 years ago. And no person can save a man today.

"Neither is there salvation in any other: for there is none other name under heaven given among men, whereby we must be saved" (Acts 4:12).

"None other name" does not mean the name of a TV minister, radio evangelist, famous author, pastor, Christian psychologist, or denominational boss. God's Word emphatically states, "none other name" but the name of Jesus.

The blind man had to learn that a religious encounter is not the answer.

The most famous quote from the story must be verse 25. This gentleman certainly had a way with words, and the hierarchy interrogating him did not intimidate him. There is a poetic flow to his response that is balanced by an undaunted boldness.

> *He answered and said, Whether he be a sinner or no, I know not: one thing I know, that, whereas I was blind, now I see.*—JOHN 9:25

Even today many sing the chorus:

> This one thing I know;
> This one thing I know;
> God in great mercy pardoned me,
> Snapped sins fetters and set me free;
> Once I was blind but now I see;
> This one thing I know![17]

There is one problem. When the man made the statement, he wasn't a saved man.

A saved man cannot say, "Whether he be a sinner or no." If Jesus were an ordinary sinner, He could not be the Saviour, and for a Jewish man in the first century to be saved, he would have to recognize Jesus as the perfect Messiah. Only God's blameless Son could wash away a man's sins.

It is very obvious the man was not saved in verse 25, because the Bible clearly tells us when he was saved. In verse 38 he cries out, "Lord, I believe," and the Word of God teaches, "Believe on the Lord Jesus Christ, and thou shalt be saved" (Acts 16:31).

Yet, in verse 25, there are a number of wonderful statements the man could claim about the glorious experience in his life. He could sing, "He touched me, and oh the joy that floods my soul. He touched me and made me whole." He could say, "Praise the Lord. I saw the light!" He could truly say that he had an "encounter with Jesus," but for all his experiences, there is an incredibly important point to understand.

"*Fix* me" is not the same as "*Save* me."

Not the same at all.

For example, consider the following—stories possibly similar to those you've experienced or heard:

A man is a slave to liquor. He is losing his job, his marriage, his family, and his health to the master of booze. He has tried prescriptions, programs, and psychologists to no avail, so in desperation, he turns to a "higher power." He is delivered with no other explanation than God doing a wonderful work in his life.

A woman is losing her life to cancer. The doctors, having done their best, give her no hope. Despondent, she turns to Jesus, pleading for His healing hand. The next week, her doctors discover in amazement that her cancer is gone. She can only praise the mercy of God for the medical miracle.

Another has a dream.

Another claims, "God spoke to me."

Another visits a weeping statue.

Another "dies" in a car accident and sojourns to Heaven.

Another gets a revelation that no one else sees.

A Google search of the words "vision of Christ" yielded more than a quarter of a million hits. Someone you know has had an *experience.*

But the Bible says there is only one way to be saved from our sins.

> *But as many as received him, to them gave he power to become the sons of God, even to them that believe on his name.*—JOHN 1:12

> *To him give all the prophets witness, that through his name whosoever believeth in him shall receive remission of sins.*—ACTS 10:43

> *For ye are all the children of God by faith in Christ Jesus.*—GALATIANS 3:26

We are not saved by experiences, encounters, or visions. We are saved through Christ. We must believe that Jesus died for our sins, that He was buried, that He rose again, and we must trust Him and only Him to wash our sins away.

There is a difference between the man who wants Jesus to fix his problem and the man who wants Jesus to save his soul. There is a difference between the woman who wants Jesus to touch her body and the woman who wants Jesus to adopt her into the family of God. There is a difference between the religious zealot who wants to get a new experience and the lost sinner who is desperate for a new heart.

We have been deceived, and we have accepted the lie. The deficient religious climate we are living in has allowed multitudes of people to accept a version of the gospel that is so diluted, their very souls are in danger of Hell. Cheap preaching that refuses to condemn sin has left them with "no fear of God before their eyes" (Romans 3:18). Because ministers would rather please man than God (Galatians 1:10), a watered-down salvation has replaced Bible salvation. The results are disastrous.

And so it was for the blind man. Step by step, the Lord Jesus had to lift the scales from his eyes. By the time the religious leaders "cast him out," he was ready for Jesus to take him in. The blinded eyes of his heart had seen the emptiness of religion, and the impotence of its leadership. The "goodness of God" had truly led him to repentance (Romans 2:4), and he was ready to understand the critical truth of the gospel.

The blind man had to learn that Jesus is the only Saviour.

It is not Christ plus religion. It is not Christ plus the minister. It is not Christ plus an experience. It is Jesus and only Jesus.

How lucid was the exchange between the blind man and the Son of God, "Jesus heard that they had cast him out; and when he had found him, he said unto him, Dost thou believe on the Son of God? He answered and said, Who is he, Lord, that I might believe on him? And Jesus said unto him, Thou hast both seen him, and it is he that talketh with thee. And he said, Lord, I believe. And he worshipped him" (John 9:35–38).

How simple is that? *"Lord I believe."*

I believe You are the Son of God.

I believe You are the only one who can take my sins away.

I believe.

In an instant, a second miracle took place—a miracle far greater and far more significant than the first miracle. His spiritual eyes were opened, and for the first time, he could truly see.

We might well imagine the magnificence of a blind man seeing for the first time in his life, but consider what happens when a spiritually blind man suddenly sees. For the first time he sees the difference between Christ and religion. He knows what it is to have the weight of a lifetime's load of sin removed from his heart. He experiences the guilt and shame that engrossed his life being summarily replaced by a peace "which passeth all understanding" (Philippians 4:7).

"And Jesus said, For judgment I am come into this world, that they which see not might see; and that they which see might be made blind" (John 9:39). There is no neutrality with Christ. Either we trust Him and He opens our eyes, or we reject Him and our spiritual blindness intensifies.

He is the master of opening blinded eyes. He heals the *one thing*.

Jesus is the light of the world.

Years ago, thousands of religious pilgrims made their way to Calcutta, India, hoping to worship and bathe in the Hooghly River. An eclipse of the sun was the occasion of their journey, and they intended to ward off evil spirits by dipping in the sacred waters. Their fear and superstition convinced them a great power in the form of a serpent was about to swallow their sun god.

From a nearby YMCA building, a gentleman named Earl Taylor witnessed the desperate act. As a countless multitude wailed, he suddenly heard a group of native Christians singing:

> The whole world was lost in the darkness of sin,
>   the light of the world is Jesus!
> Like sunshine at noonday, His glory shone in. The
>   light of the world is Jesus!

No darkness have we who in Jesus abide; the light
of the world is Jesus!
We walk in the light when we follow our guide!
The light of the world is Jesus!
Ye dwellers in darkness with sin blinded eyes, the
light of the world is Jesus!
Go, wash, at His bidding, and light will arise. The
light of the world is Jesus!
No need of the sunlight In Heaven we're told; the
light of the world is Jesus!
The Lamb is the light In the city of gold, the light
of the world is Jesus
Come to the light, 'tis shining for thee; sweetly the
light has dawned upon me.
Once I was blind, but now I can see: the light of
the world is Jesus![18]

Jesus is still opening blinded hearts. He is still
overcoming the *one thing*.

Conclusion

YOUR ONE THING

So what is your *one thing*? When the pretense is stripped away, when the religious game is over, when it is just you and God, what is the *one thing* that keeps you from trusting Christ?

Consider three questions:

Is my "one thing" more valuable than my eternal soul?

In Mark 8:36–37, Jesus asked a penetrating question: "For what shall it profit a man, if he shall gain the whole world, and lose his own soul? Or what shall a man give in exchange for his soul?" To *exchange* means "to barter," so a man facing the issue of his *one thing* is truly a man auctioning his soul.

Is alcohol more valuable than your soul? Is wealth really more valuable than your soul? Is a night of lust and sin or an illicit relationship more valuable than your soul?

What price do you put on your soul?

Myra Brooks Welch, in her beloved poem *The Touch of the Master's Hand*, wrote it perfectly:

> And many a man with life out of tune,
> And battered and scarred with sin,
> Is auctioned cheap to the thoughtless crowd,
> Much like the old violin.
>
> A "mess of pottage," a glass of wine;
> A game—and he travels on.
> He is "going" once, and "going" twice,
> He's "going" and almost "gone."
>
> But the Master comes, and the foolish crowd
> Never can quite understand
> The worth of a soul and the change that's wrought
> By the touch of the Master's hand.[19]

You stand on the auction block of eternity. At stake is your soul. Are you really willing to sell it for *one thing*? Is it that important to you?

Is my "one thing" worth going to Hell for?

Is there any sin so pleasurable, so paramount, so powerful, that it is worth the fires of Hell? While Satan paints a permissive picture of sin, and his Hollywood cohorts scoff and ridicule, and his "ministers" (2 Corinthians 11:15) discount the judgment of God, the Bible declares a different reality.

The Bible calls Hell a "furnace of fire" (Matthew 13:42), a place of "torments" (Luke 16:23), a lake of "fire and brimstone" (Revelation 20:10), and a "flaming fire" (2 Thessalonians 1:8). Many in Hell are weeping and gnashing their teeth in angry rages of pain (Matthew 24:51). They will suffer eternally as Hell is a place where the "fire is not quenched" (Mark 9:44).

There are a terrifying number of Scriptures describing the excruciating throes a lost person encounters in Hell, the sum of which should convince the hardest heart there is simply no sin, no pleasure, no *one thing* so important, it is worth risking the peril of Hell.

There remains the "wages of sin" (Romans 6:23). There still is the issue of sin "when it is finished" (James 1:15). And there stands the promise that "God is not mocked: for whatsoever a man soweth, that shall he also reap" (Galatians 6:7).

If you allow that *one thing* to keep you from trusting Christ, you are allowing that *one thing* to seal your eternal destiny in Hell.

Is my "one thing" greater than the love of Christ?

Many powerful motivations fill the Bible giving a lost man reason to come to Christ. The fear of Hell, the control of sin, the loneliness and despair of a hurting life, and the uncertainty of death, are only a few. There is, however, a motivation that is higher and greater, and it is the preeminent reason a sinner should be saved.

*For the love of Christ constraineth us; because
we thus judge, that if one died for all, then were
all dead: And that he died for all, that they which
live should not henceforth live unto themselves,
but unto him which died for them, and rose again.*
—2 CORINTHIANS 5:14–15

Words like these are nearly incomprehensible for
our feeble thinking.

*But [Jesus] made himself of no reputation, and
took upon him the form of a servant, and was
made in the likeness of men: And being found in
fashion as a man, he humbled himself, and became
obedient unto death, even the death of the cross.*
—PHILIPPIANS 2:7–8

We may be able to understand why someone
would die for a righteous man or a good man, yet the
astounding keystone of the Bible is that *"while we were
yet sinners,* Christ died for us" (Romans 5:7–8). Even
though I rebel against His commands, He died for
me. Though like a helpless lamb, I choose to go my
way and not His way, He died for me. Though I may
choose sin instead of Him, He still died for me.

As one author[20] attempted to describe God's love in poetry, he knew even as he wrote that the love of God is too vast to be conveyed through words:

> *Could we with ink the ocean fill and were the skies of parchment made,*
> *Were ev'ry stalk on earth a quill and ev'ry man a scribe by trade*
> *To write the love of God above would drain the ocean dry,*
> *Nor could the scroll contain the whole tho stretched from sky to sky.*

No human author or artist has ever adequately described the love of God. "God so loved the world" (John 3:16) transcends our rational ability to understand why He is merciful to such sinners. There is no cogent explanation. "Christ died for our sins" (1 Corinthians 15:3), and we can only stand amazed!

Will you reject that love? Can you remain calloused to Him, indifferent to the sacrifice of the cross for you? When you see Jesus enduring the excruciating slaughter at the hands of human beings for you, is it nothing to you? If the love of Calvary cannot warm your heart, what will?

What *one thing* could possibly overshadow Him?

There is one more "one thing."

The date was December 7, 1941 at 07:49. Lieutenant Commander Mitsuo Fuchida of the Japanese First Air Fleet was flying past Barber's Point on the island of Oahu in command of the infamous attack on Pearl Harbor. Certain he had caught the Americans by surprise, at 07:53 he grabbed the radio and shouted, "Tora! Tora! Tora!"—the coded message informing the Japanese high command of their success. Hailed as a national hero, Fuchida thirsted for more, and through the course of World War II, he would lead multiple assaults throughout the Pacific dodging death at every turn.

It was a Sunday afternoon, August 5, 1945, when Fuchida, working in the city of Hiroshima, received orders to fly to Yamato. Within the hour, the city was behind him as he flew alone in a Navy three-seater aircraft. He landed two hours later, not realizing that

God had spared his life yet again. The next morning, an atomic bomb destroyed Hiroshima.

As the war continued, the fortunes of Mitsuo Fuchida changed. Once proclaimed a national legend, Fuchida was blamed for the loss to the Americans, leaving him an embittered man. Forced to witness at war crime tribunals, he became obsessed with hatred towards his many enemies. The Soviets, the Australians, and the Americans were all suitable targets for his wrath.

That resentment became his *one thing.*

The trials bore witness to horrific atrocities Americans had suffered at the hands of their Japanese captors. Convinced there was another side to this story, Fuchida determined to collect evidence proving his contention. He would attend the next tribunal, shove the documented charges into the judges' faces, claiming the Americans were no different.

In the spring of 1947, 150 prisoners were returning to Japan from the United States. Fuchida, desiring to hear their accounts of imprisonment in POW camps, went to the Uraga Harbor near Yokosuka. First off the ships were the sick and injured, then, much to his amazement, a former colleague named Kazuo Kanegasaki disembarked. Stunned, he told him, "Everyone thought you were dead! A tombstone has been erected in your honor in Tokyo!"

Kanegasaki, amused by the spectacle of viewing his own tombstone, explained that when his ship was sunk, he spent thirteen days in a lifeboat before being rescued by the Americans. Ashamed at being captured, he gave a false name, and was never correctly reported as a prisoner.

His countrymen assumed he had died at sea, and a tomb was erected in his memory. Four years later, even his wife had given up hope and had remarried, yet he was very much alive. Imprisoned in San Diego, he tried to starve himself to death, but the authorities kept him alive by injections. A pastor from Los Angeles was called to counsel Kanegasaki, and persuaded him that life still had meaning.

Transferred to a camp on the Colorado/Utah border for the remainder of the war, his life was transformed. There he met a woman named Peggy

Covell who treated the prisoners with gracious care, offering to help in any way possible. Her kindness so impressed them, one of the prisoners finally asked, "Why are you so kind to us?" They were stunned by her answer.

"Because Japanese soldiers killed my parents."

Her parents had been teachers at a religious school in Yokohama. At the outbreak of the war, the Covells fled to Manila, but when the Japanese invaded, they escaped to the mountains of the north. When the Americans chased the Japanese out of Manila, they fled to the same mountains. They discovered the missionaries and their radio, tried them as spies, and beheaded them.

When Peggy heard of her parents' fate, she was choked with hatred for the Japanese. But as she contemplated her parents' concern and service for them, she was convinced that even in their dying moments they still loved their captors, and she could do the same. She volunteered countless hours ministering to and working with Japanese POW's in the States.

The story stunned Mitsuo Fuchida. He had come to get dirt, yet instead, he heard a powerful story of mercy. He interviewed every prisoner he could find who had met Peggy Covell and was amazed at such love. She had what Fuchida was seeking. The bitterness, revenge, and hatred that poisoned his soul was the polar opposite of the compassionate forgiveness of Peggy Covell. He needed what she had!

He purchased a New Testament, reading two or three chapters a day, and then pondering its message. Slowly, yet surely, the words of God burned in his heart. The conviction of sin grew, and in September of 1949, Fuchida came to Luke 23. As he read the story of Calvary and the horrible death of Christ, he stopped at these words: "Then said Jesus, Father, forgive them; for they know not what they do" (Luke 23:34).

Tears filled his eyes as he reached the end of what he called a "long wandering." Christ not only died for the world, He died for Mitsuo Fuchida. That's why Mr. and Mrs. Covell were willing to sacrifice their lives at the hands of the people they loved. That is the reason that Peggy Covell could graciously serve a people most would have detested. The Saviour desired to forgive an angry, bitter warrior, and—captivated by the love of Calvary—Fuchida trusted Jesus to wash his sins away. Mitsuo Fuchida would spend his final years preaching the transforming power of Christ.[21]

Jesus conquered his *one thing*.

Will you surrender your "one thing"?

Through the corridor of time, individuals like Nicodemus, the woman of Samaria, and the blind man of Jerusalem have placed their *one thing* on one side of the balance, and the love of God on the other side. Men like Mel Trotter and Mitsuo Fuchida, controlled by their own personal *one thing*, have surrendered to the mercy of Jesus, trusting Him to save their souls. They discovered that their *one thing* wasn't as important as they had thought. Amazed by the mercy of Christ, how could they do less than surrender their *one thing* and trust Him!

What is your *one thing*? What keeps you from trusting Christ today? And what will it take before you surrender to His mercy?

Are you ready to surrender your *one thing* and turn to the one Person who can give you more than that *one thing* ever could?

Would you trust Him today? Give up your *one thing* with one simple call. Romans 10:13 promises, "For whosoever shall call upon the name of the Lord shall be saved."

———————————

If you have chosen to place your faith in Christ alone through reading this book, I would love to hear from you. You can contact me through Striving Together Publications by sending a message to onething@strivingtogether.com.

Notes

1. Charles Chiniquy, *Fify Years in the Church of Rome* (CreateSpace Independent Publishing Platform, 2013), 415.

2. Ibid., 418.

3. *Hallelujah, What a Saviour!* Words & Music: Philip P. Bliss, in International Lessons Monthly, 1875.

4. Gerald L. Borchert, *The New American Commentary, Vol. 25A: John 1–11* (B & H Publishing Group, 1996), 202.

5. Ibid., 206.

6. Andreas J. Köstenberger, *John: Baker Exegetical Commentary on the New Testament* (Grand Rapids, MI: Baker Academic, 2004), 152.

7. Sharon Epperson and Karina Frayter, "More Unmarried Couples Living Together in Retirement," USA Today, April 10, 2011, Money section, http://usatoday30.usatoday.com/money/perfi/retirement/2011-04-10-cnbc-unmarried-couples-in-retirement-together.htm.

8. John Curtis, "Advantages of Cohabitation," http://goarticles.com/article/Advantages-of-Cohabitation/1494297/.

9. Scott Reeves, "Living Together Makes More Sense Than Marriage," Forbes, August 3, 2005, Financial Planning section, http://www.forbes.com/2005/08/03/marriage-finances-money-cx_sr_0803middleage.html.

10. John Phillips, *Exploring the Gospel of John* (Grand Rapids, MI: Kregel Publications, 2001), 87.

11. *All I Need.* Words and Music: Charles P. Jones. 1906

12. Leona Hertel, *Man With a Mission* (Grand Rapids, MI: Kregel Publications, 2001).

13. Smith, Oswald J. *Then Jesus Came.* The Rodeheaver Company. 1940

14. B. M. Newman and E. A. Nida, *A Translator's Handbook on the Gospel of John* (United Bible Societies, 1980), 297–298.

15. Jim Bishop, *The Day Christ Died* (HarperOne, 1991), 31.

16. Colin G. Kruse, *The Gospel According to John: An Introduction and Commentary* (Eerdmans Publishing Company, 2004), 223.

17. This One Thing I Know. *Salvation Army Songbook 347.*

18. *The Light of the World is Jesus.* Words and Music: Phillip P. Bliss. Story from www.cyberhymnal.org

19. Bernard Jensen, *The Joy of Living and How to Attain It* (Kessinger Publishing, 2006), 271.

20. Commonly ascribed to Frederick M. Lehman, but first penned by Meir Ben Isaac Nehorai.

21. Gordon W. Prange, *God's Samurai* (Riverside, NJ: Macmillian Publishing Co., 1990).

Also available from
Striving Together Publications

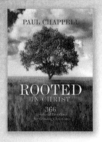

Rooted in Christ
Paul Chappell
In this power-packed daily devotional, each page beckons you to a deeper relationship with God, helping you discover for yourself the life-changing power of His unshakable love. As each brief reading draws you to the Lord, you'll be equipped to greet each day with bold faith, confident in God's faithfulness, strength, and transforming grace. (424 pages, hardback)

Living Beyond Your Capacity
Paul Chappell
The wonderful Holy Spirit of God desires to come into your life at salvation and unfold a daily work of power, grace, and transformation. He can enable you to live a supernatural life—a life that exceeds your human capacity. You can begin discovering and experiencing the Spirit-filled life today! (208 pages, paperback)

Done.
Cary Schmidt
Specifically created to be placed into the hands of an unsaved person and a perfect gift for first time church visitors, this minibook explains the gospel in crystal clear terms. The reader will journey step by step through biblical reasoning that concludes at the cross and a moment of decision. (112 pages, mini-paperback)

strivingtogether.com

Visit us online

strivingtogether.com

wcbc.edu